SELF HELP BOOKS

The 101 Best Personal Development Classics

Vic Johnson

Laurenzana Press
Melrose FL

SELF HELP BOOKS:
The 101 Best Personal Development Classics
Vic Johnson

Get a FREE Smart Goals Worksheet and Video
http://www.Get-Smart-Goals.com

Published by:
Laurenzana Press
PO Box 1220
Melrose, FL 32666 USA
www.LaurenzanaPress.com

Book design by Sue Balcer, justyourtype.biz

ISBN-13 : 978-1-937918-36-1

Table of Contents

Introduction

When my youngest son turned twenty we had a party at our house to celebrate the occasion. Most of the guests were friends of his who were in his age group.

Late in the afternoon I went downstairs and found my son huddled up with several of his friends and his football coach from high school. They were sitting on the porch in front of my library that has an incredible view overlooking the lake and loads of wildlife that hang out there.

The conversation very quickly turned to "wealth" and what it must have taken to acquire "such a place."

When I asked the young twenty-something who posed the question if he'd like to see what created all that wealth, an incredulous and eager look came over his face as he nodded affirmingly.

I then pointed toward the glass to direct their attention to my library behind them and said, "Those books bought this house and everything in it." Then I shared one of my favorite Jim Rohn quotes with them, "Poor people have big TV's in their homes. Rich people have big libraries in theirs."

Whereupon the questioner instantly recognized the simplicity of that wisdom, but in a moment seemed perplexed when he said, "But Mr. J you've got seven televisions in your house." To which I replied, "And every one of them were bought with those books, and not the other way around."

Thus has been the impact of books on my life, especially personal development books, and especially the personal development books you're about to read about.

They literally "saved my life." Even during the days when my family and I were evicted from our home, lost the last automobile we had and qualified below the federal poverty level. Even then, I had the faith that I would find the answers I needed to overcome that in these books. And indeed I did.

Now I call these the *101 Best Personal Development Classics* and I'm sure some will disagree with me. And that's fine. Part of personal growth is realizing that others may be on a different part of their path than you're on. Because of that, their perspective will certainly be different than yours.

So no doubt there will be books that some people think should have made the list. And some that didn't make it that some will insist should be listed. But I don't believe there's a single book on my list that someone wouldn't get some benefit from. And I believe most people will have some major "aha" moments from most of these books if they've never read them.

Now some people will be quick to say that the Bible is the best personal development book and should have made the list. And they're correct. And so is the Torah and the Koran and other religious texts. The principles of personal development are not new. They are as old as humans and that's why you find the principles in the written works from the very beginning.

But I have chosen to focus on some more "contemporary" but "classic" works. The oldest book I reference was first published in 1854 (Henry David Thoreau's *Walden*) and there are several books as recent as 2001-2002. In all cases these are books that have stood the test of time as humans over the years have sought them for answers.

I know some people will want to know where to start and that's a reasonable question though the truth is it really depends on where you're at on your path right now. I read *Think and Grow Rich* the first time when I was in my twenties and I couldn't figure out why everybody made such a big fuss about the book. When I read it twenty years later I would have sworn that the book had been changed since I first read it. In my forties I was ready for the wisdom that I couldn't see when I was in my twenties.

So where to start? Choose one of my top five classics and read the first two chapters. If it's not resonating with you, put it down and pick up another. And that's a wonderful thing about most personal development classics. You can pick one up, read a chapter and put it down for months. When you pick it up again it's not difficult to resume reading because there's seldom a plot to worry about following. Here's the list to choose from:

- *As A Man Thinketh*
- *How To Win Friends and Influence People*
- *Make Your Life Worthwhile*
- *The Magic of Thinking Big*
- *Think and Grow Rich*

It also wouldn't be a bad move to put Mortimer Adler's famous *How To Read a Book* near the top of your list. It'll make the rest of your reading many times more valuable.

If you've never been a reader let me give you a simple exercise that will turn you into one. In the beginning spend fifteen minutes a day, every day, reading. Some people do it first thing upon rising in the morning, others do it just before retiring in the evening. I know of people who buy used paperbacks and everyday tear out a few pages, stick it in their lunch box and read on their lunch break.

The important thing is to DO IT! After a few weeks it becomes habit just like brushing your teeth. The more you read the more you'll want to extend your reading time. Eventually you'll be reading thirty minutes to an hour a day. When you're doing that EVERY day, some amazing things will begin happening in your life.

So without further ado, let's get started with the 101 Best Personal Development Classics!

Attention All Eagle Eyes: We've had a number of people proof this book before we released it to you, but there is a chance you might spot something that was missed. If you find a typo or other obvious error please send it to us. And if you're the first one to report it, we'll send you a free gift! Send to: corrections@laurenzanapress.com

Acres Of Diamonds (1890)

Russell H. Conwell
Major Theme: Spirituality and happiness

Acres of Diamonds actually started as a speech given by Russell H. Conwell in order to raise money for the newly formed Temple University. Before he was finished, Conwell would deliver the talk more than 6,000 times. It eventually made its way into print where it has become a classic with the timeless message that you can find wealth, happiness, and success right within your own current circumstances.

For anyone who feels like they're stuck in the rat race, constantly chasing the next biggest item on their to-buy list, this book can help you re-evaluate your life's goals and teach you that happiness truly does come from within.

This is a very small book and a quick read and makes a wonderful selection for a weekend when weather keeps you in.

As A Man Thinketh (1902)

James Allen
Major Theme: Personal fulfillment and the power of the mind

This book by James Allen is based on the premise that your life, and everything in it, is entirely shaped by your perception of it and your thoughts as you go about your day. Thus, one of the primary goals of this book is to teach the reader how to train the mind to think in patterns that bring about success, health, happiness, and joy.

This is the little book that's most responsible for you reading the one you're currently reading. Had I not read *As A Man Thinketh* I might not have gone on to the success I've had, which led to me becoming an author.

In 2001 I created a website with the specific purpose of giving this book away. As I write this we're closing in on more than a half million copies distributed. If you'd like a free copy (we give you three different versions so you can read on a Kindle, iPad, Nook and most other eBook readers) you can download one here: www.AsAManThinketh.net

Millions of people have been influenced by James Allen's work and most personal development teachers quote extensively from the book. Mark Victor Hansen, co-author of the Chicken Soup books, says he's read it more than 25 times. The legendary Og Mandino called it one of the top ten books of all time.

Very definitely should be on your short list to read if you've never read it before.

Atlas Shrugged (1957)

Ayn Rand
Major Theme: The role of man's mind in existence

In this world-renowned book, Ayn Rand takes a closer look into the primary drives and motives of society and how these are slowly leading to its collapse. The book offers hope to those who feel stuck in their current life situation and shows them how to create change by reshaping the way they look at their situation and making change from within.

This book is based around the concept that facts are facts but it is reason that determines your success and happiness. You can be in any situation and still achieve a sense of inner joy and peace provided you look at your circumstance in the correct manner and are searching for fulfillment from within rather than from outwardly possessions or factors.

Unlike most of the personal development classics, this is a fiction book and much longer than most. I wouldn't make this one of my first choices. Wait until you've become a more accomplished reader and you've got some of these other volumes under your belt. You'll appreciate Atlas Shrugged a lot more.

Awaken The Giant Within (1992)

Anthony Robbins
Major Theme: Self-thought and its impact on health, happiness, and success

In this book, Anthony Robbins takes a closer look at how you can go about mastering your emotions to ensure that you are making the most of your existence and creating a life that is filled with happiness, joy, and self-confidence.

He takes a look at key strategies that you can use to enhance your relationships, turn your financial situation around, and how to improve your health so that you feel better on a daily basis. He's a big believer that improved physical energy makes you far more effective in all you do.

This book is highly focused on the concept of self-mastery and special techniques you can use to "empower yourself."

Chicken Soup For The Soul (1993)

Mark Victor Hansen and Jack Canfield
Major Theme: Happiness and Inspiration

Perhaps the most successful book series ever, *Chicken Soup For The Soul* is well-known by many. And, if you haven't read the original version, there's a good chance that you may have read another variety in the series as over 200 further editions have come out since original publication targeting readers of all audiences.

The first book in the series provides powerful essays and stories of happiness, motivation, and selfless deeds that others have contributed, as told by motivational speakers Mark Victor Hansen and Jack Canfield. By reading through it you'll gain a higher sense of humanity and help to see that happiness is really possible across so many situations.

Just as the name implies, this book, and the others in the series are like "chicken soup" when you're ailing on the inside. This is a great book to keep on the nightstand where you can pick it up, read a story and fall asleep with the comfort of knowing tomorrow will be a better day.

Don't Sweat The Small Stuff (1997)

Richard Carlson
Major Theme: Stress reduction and appreciation

If you're someone who constantly finds yourself stressed out each and every day, *Don't Sweat the Small Stuff* is a terrific book to explore to help put you in a more peaceful state of mind and learn to let go of the little things that you feel 'drive you crazy'.

Very many of us often get wrapped up in the mundane events of the day which can dampen the spirit and kill your inner joy. Richard Carlson teaches you how to quiet those inner stressful voices that show up after little events causing you this feeling of sadness so you can free yourself to focus on the more important matters in your life – what does bring you happiness and fulfillment.

This book will teach you to live your life with more gratitude and appreciation while learning to place more emphasis on generosity and non-material things.

Even Eagles Need A Push (1990)

David McNally
Major Theme: Self-change and learning the true value of happiness

In this book, David McNally takes a deeper look into what it really means to be happy and how you can shape your reality to help foster greater feelings of joy, self-esteem and confidence, and become the best you that you can be.

He shares with you how to assess where you are today in comparison with where you want to be going and then helps you learn the key strategies that you should be focusing on putting into place to shape your existence.

He'll teach you to look carefully at what really matters most to you and gain insight on how to place more focus on these areas of your life while not letting other elements that take away from your joy and happiness shape who you are coming to be.

Failing Forward: Turning Mistakes Into Stepping Stones For Success (2000)

John Maxwell
Major Theme: Self-Belief and mindset

In this powerful book, John Maxwell illustrates to you that true success does not come from all the various achievements that you've made in life, but rather comes from being able to learn from your past mistakes and move forward from them, using the experience to shape your future.

Those who have the ability to put their failures behind them and overcome their fears so that they can face the future with the right mind frame and desire to succeed are going to be the ones who obtain optimal success in their life.

John provides a number of different exercises that can be done to help you learn the secret to being able to move beyond problems that you encounter and direct your focus forward onto using the experience to fuel future change.

I've read a number of Maxwell's books and seen him speak several times. This is one of his best works and I often recommend it to others because I think failure is such a big obstacle to most people.

There's no question that successful people view failure differently than unsuccessful people. I even teach that successful people are bigger failures and it's true. It's how they become successful – by continuing to persist even when things don't go according to plan. This is a great book to convince you of that logical argument!

Feel The Fear And Do It Anyway (1987)

Susan Jeffers
Major Theme: Self-belief and mastery

From my own personal experience I believe that fear has killed more dreams and ambitions and sentenced more people to a miserable life than any other single cause. I could easily call unmanaged fear the number one enemy of mankind.

In this book, Susan Jeffers teaches you how to unearth what it is that you fear in life and how to overcome those fears so that you can enhance your existence, achieving all the success and dreams that you've set out to.

Each of us has our own unique fears that prevent us from becoming who we truly want to be. It's only those who are able to identify these fears and take powerful steps to get beyond them that will see the changes in life that they want to create.

Jeffers provides you with a 10-step process for retrainning

your mind to become more positive and face your fears head on so that they don't prevent you from trying new experiences in life and achieving a state of complete happiness.

First Things First (1994)

Stephen Covey
Major Theme: Time management

If you're constantly harried by time, seeming always to feel that you're running at full speed just to keep up, *First Things First* should be at the top of your list to read.

Covey helps you learn how to properly manage your time in this book so that you can put more focus and emphasis on the things that really matter most to you. The magic is in a quadrant that he describes in a very simple and easy-to-understand way. You can immediately grasp why you're struggling now and you'll easily see the changes you need to make.

In the quadrant exercise you carefully identify different elements of your life to determine whether they are important and urgent, important and not urgent, urgent but not important, along with not urgent and not important so that you know precisely where your time is best spent.

I've had a lot of people report back with very positive results after I recommended this to them for reading.

Five Major Pieces To The Life Puzzle (1991)

Jim Rohn
Major Theme: Attitude and self-belief corrections

In his book, *Five Major Pieces To The Life Puzzle*, Jim Rohn looks at why some people are more happy and successful than others – namely, they have five key areas of their life working for them in a way that establishes a proper frame of mind that breeds further success.

This is classic Rohn and if you've never read or heard of Jim before, this is a great introduction. He discusses the fact that our personal philosophy is what will guide our own attitude about everything that happens on a daily basis and it's this attitude that shapes our future actions.

He also talks about strategies that you can do to help improve your attitude so that you perceive your environment differently and are able to find the success and inner joy that you're striving for all while striking a better balance in your day-to-day life.

Another book of Jim's that focuses on the importance of having a personal philosophy is *My Philosophy for Successful Living*. It didn't make this list because it's a more recent book. But it too is classic Rohn and a great quick read.

Getting Things Done (2001)

David Allen
Major Theme: Time Management

This is the only other Time Management book I consider to be in the same class as Covey's *First Things First.* Perhaps a bit more technique oriented, you'll definitely be making changes after this read.

Allen walks you through tips and techniques to reassess your goals and stay focused so that you avoid taking too long to complete a task you're working on as well as shows you how to overcome feelings of confusion, anxiety, and being overwhelmed.

For anyone who is often stressed because they don't have enough time, this is the book for you.

How I Raised Myself From Failure To Success In Selling (1947)

Frank Bettger
Major Theme: Sales techniques and inspiration

In this book, you'll learn the personal story of Frank Bettger and how he transformed himself into a top salesman, creating the career he had dreamed of.

He'll teach you how to harness the power of enthusiasm, overcome your fears so you can face obstacles head on, and how to win confidence in those who you are attempting to sell to.

In addition to this, he'll also go over his seven golden rules for closing a sale so you have some strong actionable steps to take to achieve success in this field. If you sell anything (and don't we all sell something) this should be at the top of your list.

How To Get What You Want (1917)

Orison Swett Marden
Major Theme: Personal Development and fulfillment

Orison Swett Marden was a prolific personal development writer and after I was introduced to his works I quickly became convinced he is one of the top five writers of the last 150 years.

Marden was the founder of the original *Success* magazine and grew it to 500,000 subscribers in the late 19th century, an incredible number for that time. In this book he illustrates the keys to finally realizing happiness and success in your life by taking control over the factors that you have available to you right now and using them to your advantage to achieve the goals you've set for yourself.

You'll learn how to overcome obstacles that cross your path and remain positive despite any setbacks that you might encounter so that you can push onwards to the results that you desire.

How To Have Confidence And Power In Dealing With People (1956)

Les Giblin
Major Theme: Confidence and influence

Most everyone reading this book will probably have heard of Dale Carnegie's *How To Win Friends and Influence People.* It's one of the top selling books of all time and it's listed elsewhere in this book. But to tell you the truth, I probably learned as much from Giblin's book as I did from Carnegie's. It seems to be a little simpler to understand and I found it easier to relate to.

Giblin teaches you how to gain an inner sense of self-confidence that you then reveal to others, helping to influence them in the way that you are hoping for. This book will help you come to understand why up to 90 percent of people fail in their life and what the real keys to happiness are.

In addition to that, he'll also explain the basic secret that you must know for influencing others so that you can make and keep friends, succeed in business and your career, and become well-liked by your peers.

He'll finish up by teaching you some quick techniques for winning arguments, how to improve your brain-power and how to criticize others without offending them. Make this one of the first twenty books or so that you read.

How To Read A Book (1940)

Mortimer J. Adler
Major Theme: Reading and comprehension

For anyone who loves the written word, this book will guide you through how to make the most of your reading experience and take home all the information that any book is trying to give you.

Whether you're reading fiction, educational material,

personal development or reference books, this book will guide you through techniques that you can use to master the skill of reading.

You'll also gain tips on how to increase the speed in which you read so that you can cover more ground quickly and increase your knowledge base. In addition to that, you'll find out how to enhance your reading comprehension so that you retain more of what you've read, really gaining from the learning experience.

As I noted in the introduction, it wouldn't be a bad idea to make this one of your early reads as it will help you tremendously with reading and comprehending the others.

How To Stop Worrying And Start Living (1944)

Dale Carnegie
Major Theme: Stress and worry reduction

The next two books are the best books written by Dale Carnegie, a hugely successful author who I don't think ever wrote a bad book.

If you often find yourself highly stressed out and worried about events taking place in your life, this book by Carnegie can help you put things into perspective. In it he reveals a number of personal stories told by historical figures and business leaders on how to overcome worry and move forward with your life.

He provides you with practical information for escaping the worry trap and getting beyond your fears to accomplish what it is that is truly meaningful to you. In addition to this, he also illustrates how you can avoid fatigue and how you can add one hour to each and every day simply by reducing worry and using effective time management strategies.

You're offered a practical formula to follow so regardless of your situation, you can benefit from this book.

How To Win Friends And Influence People (1936)

Dale Carnegie
Major Theme: Interpersonal relationships

If you feel as though your social life or your career connections could use a bit of a boost, *How To Win Friends And Influence People* is a great book to venture into. This book is one of the top personal development books of all time and has sold over 15 million copies worldwide. Thousands of people have put the strategies described in this book to good use to gain power over their lives and breed a higher level of confidence and success in dealing with others.

It is widely regarded as the gold standard among books teaching people how to create and improve interpersonal relationships. Carnegie teaches you how to influence those you come into contact with without having them feel manipulated so that you can achieve the desired results you're looking for and form stronger social bonds.

For anyone who is looking to improve interactions with others, this is a must-read.

Hung By The Tongue (1979)

Francis P. Martin
Major Theme: Faith and personal development

There's one person in the world who listens to every word you say – whether you say them out loud or to yourself (self talk). It's your sub-conscious of course and the result of hearing all those words can be amazing.

In *Hung By The Tongue* Martin teaches us the power of our words and illustrates the connection between how you speak and what you feel and how this all will influence the type of life you'll end up with.

He talks about the fact that your successes or failures are really pre-determined by your mind and come out through the words and actions you take, motivating you to see that the power of change is possible with the right steps forward.

This book has strong Christian faith references so anyone who is spiritual and looking to improve their quality of life and frame of mind will benefit from it.

I Dare You (1931)

William H. Danforth
Major Theme: Personal Growth And Development

Very few of us ever challenge the status quo and dare to step out of our comfort zones and realize all that we are capable of. This book, *I Dare You*, by William H. Danforth, will change your thinking, inspire you to create change, and possibly alter the course of your life.

Danforth talks about pushing your boundaries in all elements of your life including your sense of adventure, your motivation to take action in your life rather than be a passive bystander, your desire to be strong and creative, as well as your ability to build a magnetic personality and strong character.

The centerpiece of his training is the four quadrants of your life that he proposed needed to be in balance to live a happy and productive life. He would illustrate this in a checkerboard fashion and the checkerboard eventually became the logo of the company he founded, Ralston Purina (now Nestle Purina).

In Tune With The Infinite (1910)

Ralph Waldo Trine
Major Theme: Personal achievement and development

If you're looking for happiness in material possessions and instead have found frustration, discouragement and depression, you're ready for *In Tune With The Infinite.*

Trine will guide you through your own self-reflection on what matters most in the world, allowing you to identify where you should be devoting your time and efforts for achieving the greatest degree of success.

This book will teach you how to obtain inner peace and clarity as you move through the hectic pace of your busy life and how to value the power of life to a larger extent.

It Works! (1926)

R.H. Jarrett
Major Theme: Self-Improvement

It doesn't always take a lot of words to get the point across! If you want a light and fast read that will make a difference in your life, *It Works!* By R.H. Jarrett has already done it for millions. This book, nothing more than a pamphlet really, will help you learn a very firm set of rules to follow for obtaining all of your desires in life and making the most of your current situation.

It doesn't matter where you currently are, Jarrett firmly believes that with the right actionable steps you can overcome your current circumstance and create the life that you want to live.

If you want some QUICK inspiration, motivation, and a little bit of extra courage, this is the book for you.

Learned Optimism (1990)

Martin Seligman
Major Theme: Self-Improvement and the power of thought

In *Learned Optimism* Seligman teaches that there are basically two ways that you can look at life and the way in which you currently see your world will have an immediate influence on how you live and the success that you see.

He talks about what it means to feel helpless and how you can overcome these feelings and take back control and power in your own life.

He also talks about seeing success at work, school, sports, maintaining good health, and how to foster a higher level of optimism in children for any readers who also happen to be parents.

If you're tired of feeling like you're stuck in a rut and nothing is going your way, this book can help you break free from this and give you an entirely new look at life.

Life Is Tremendous (1968)

Charlie "Tremendous" Jones
Major Theme: Self-Improvement and view point

In this book, Tremendous Jones shares with you his personal story and techniques for changing the way that you view life and everything that happens to you so that you can foster a higher level of success, happiness, and sense of accomplishment.

This is not a big book so it's a quick read. When I read it the first time I loved every page so much that I was disappointed when it was over so quickly. But Charlie (who was one of my mentors), and this book, led me to make many changes in my life.

There is a big focus on developing a few key character traits that help to improve an individual's state of happiness and help them become a natural leader that fosters higher levels of success in the work environment. The enthusiasm with which he writes is so contagious it will have you bounding out of bed on the mornings after you read this.

You'll love Charlie's stories and the simplicity of his message. If you're a Christian you'll also appreciate his Faith which he constantly shared throughout his life and is apparent in his writing.

Live Your Dreams (1992)

Les Brown
Major Theme: Self-Power and Fulfillment

I saw Les speak during some really down times in my life and I still have the notes I wrote that kept me going from day-to-day. This book is an expansion of those ideas and a perfect fit if you've hit that place where you're wondering if anything good is ever going to happen in your life.

Les illustrates how you can find the power to change from within and how your motivation can propel you forward to achieve the greatness that you seek. He also provides you with four actionable steps that you can take immediately upon reading them to start making greater improvements in your life and well-being while reaching all the goals that you have set for yourself.

In addition to that, it also shows you how you can change your focus of your daily events so they better align with the achievements that you hope to reach while also overcoming fears that stand in your way.

Finally, he goes over how you can rid yourself of any toxic thoughts that are limiting your success and holding you back. You'll love his teaching and you'll be inspired by his own story of overcoming.

Make Your Life Worthwhile (1942)

Emmet Fox
Major Theme: Self-Development and Improvement

At a garage sale my former wife purchased a copy of *Make Your Life Worthwhile*, by the late Emmet Fox, because "it looked like a book you'd be interested in." I cannot imagine where I would be today if she hadn't gone to that garage sale. I was at the lowest point in my life, depressed beyond description. Like a person who hasn't had water in several days, I drank in page after page, almost reading the entire book in one sitting.

The change wasn't instantaneous but the book became one of my crutches for "the trip back." I read from it daily for more than two years and its impact on my life is immeasurable.

This book poses some key questions that you can ask yourself to determine how you are currently living and where there is room for improvement. You'll come to learn the many lies that people tell themselves and how this hinders their own personal growth and development so that these won't influence you in a similar manner.

Fox was a New Thought minister, with a huge following in New York City, so all of his works have strong spiritual messages, which I found to be very powerful. Interestingly, Fox's secretary had ties to the early leadership of Alcoholics Anonymous. His works were embraced by AA Co-Founder Bill W. and to this day are used by many in the organization.

Man's Search For Himself (1953)

Rollo May
Major Theme: Self-Discovery

In this book, Rollo May shares with you the path you need to take to gain an inner sense of discovery while you learn exactly who you are and what you have to offer the world.

May explains that one of the primary needs of man is to feel as though he is a contribution to society, but yet very few of us really have identified our true reason for being. As a result, this leads to feelings of loneliness, boredom, as well as emptiness that never seem to let up.

After reading this book and performing some self-reflection, you'll help to rid yourself of these feelings and feel more complete as an individual.

Man's Search For Meaning (1959)

Victor Frankl
Major Theme: Purposeful living

Victor Frankl was in a Nazi concentration camp for five years and watched all those he knew, along with many others, die right before his eyes. During that experience he developed an incredible understanding of life and how to deal with it.

He shares his experiences and some of his own innermost thoughts, needs, and desires during his confinement to help you learn how to make the most of your own life.

He then goes on to describe what he believes are the primary forces that drive us to continue living in today's world and how you can make the most of your own life to achieve fulfillment and happiness.

If you're a fan of inspirational autobiographies this one should be near the top of your list.

Maximum Achievement (1993)

Brian Tracy
Major Theme: Personal Achievement and Power

If you're someone who is looking to master many different areas of your life, this will be a good book to read to help you do so. Brian Tracy is going to take you through the seven laws of mental mastery so that you can learn what you need to do in order to create the life that you want.

He'll be discussing how to master your mind, your skills, how to gain power in your life, as well as how to make any decision as you go about your life.

He'll also provide you with sound advice on how to master human relationships, as well as personal relationships with those who you hold near and dear. Finally, he'll give some great advice on mastering the art of parenting, teaching you how to raise healthy and confident children.

Brian has long been an ardent student of success so his teachings are always very instructive. *Maximum Achievement* is one of his best examples of that.

Men Are From Mars, Women Are From Venus (1992)

John Gray
Major Theme: Relationship development

If you ever feel as though you can't understand members of the opposite sex, especially those closest to you, this book is for you. In this relationship-building book, you'll learn the main differences between males and females that make them unique and how you can use these differences to foster a healthier relationship.

You'll see how the needs, wants, and desires of the two genders differ and how this can come to strongly influence the state of any interpersonal relationships that you have.

You'll be taught key techniques for understanding your partner better so that you can foster a fulfilling relationship that is filled with understanding and respect. This book assesses both the female and male viewpoints, so is a good read for both genders to strengthen your relationships.

Wouldn't be a bad idea to buy your significant other their own copy when you get yours.

Message To Garcia (1914)

Elbert Hubbard
Major Theme: Personal Initiative and Inspiration

This book, which is really just a pamphlet, is one of pure inspiration as you'll read about a personal essay written by a soldier who is doing everything he can to accomplish his assigned mission during the Spanish-American War.

This essay outlines how he feels and thinks throughout his journey that brings him to achieve a high state of success. He doesn't ask any questions or make any objections to the tasks that are asked of him – he simply carries through with what he is supposed to do.

Message to Garcia shows you how initiative and perseverance can help you attain success in even the most trying of life's situations and will give you a sense of self-control and power to take charge of your own life and accomplish your own personal missions. Amazingly this little pamphlet has sold more than 40 million copies yet remains unknown to most.

Over The Top (1994)

Zig Ziglar
Major Theme: Self-Development and success

I first heard about and read one of Zig's books when I was in my early twenties and it had a remarkable impact on my life. That book is now called *See You At The Top* and was his first big best-seller (described later in this book).

Over The Top is pure Zig as only Zig can teach. You'll learn how the right attitude and skill set can help you attain a higher level of personal success in all elements of your life.

Those who accept that they are the creators of their

own destiny feel far more self-empowered to create the changes that they're looking for and can go on to build an "over the top" life.

Many of the principles I've learned, use and teach about achieving goals I learned from Zig. And you're going to get that great teaching in this book. Finally, you'll learn key strategies and techniques for dealing with difficult times to ensure that you stay on your path to maximum personal development.

Power Of Your Supermind (1967)

Vernon Howard
Major Theme: Personal growth

Bob Proctor first introduced me to Vernon Howard about 1999 when he sent me *Power of Your Supermind*. Howard discusses his own personal journey through improving his life and becoming the person that he wanted to be. He illustrates to you how powerful your mind can be when looking to create the success and happiness you're striving for and teaches you how to harness your own thoughts and tilt them to work in your favor.

You'll come to learn that any human problem that you may be facing can be overcome with the right mindset and action plan, making this a very empowering book that can get you through any difficult times that you may be facing.

Howard has somewhat of a "cult" following but I'm sure a lot of it results from his excellent ability to communicate great ideas to readers of his books!

Power Of Constructive Thinking (1932)

Emmet Fox
Major Theme: Positive thought

Here's another Emmet Fox book. In my opinion not quite as good as *Make Your Life Worthwhile* but still a life-changing book that should be on your list because it's classic Fox teaching.

In this book he illustrates how your thought patterns and real life existence align and influence each other. He proclaims that it is impossible to think one thing and produce another; therefore in order to lead the most successful and harmonious life you're seeking, you need to get your thoughts in line with your desired results.

He discusses how lies will eat away at your personal truth and cause feelings of unhappiness to develop as you won't feel in unity with your life as a whole.

The book has a large spiritual basis as he talks about how you can change your life through prayer and how connecting your mind and body through the regular practice of yoga will help to enhance your overall well-being. As I mentioned earlier in writing about *Make Your Life Worthwhile,* Fox was a New Thought minister, so that's why you see the spiritual emphasis. I don't see it as an obstacle but actually is part of what makes this book a must-read.

Prosperity (1936)

Charles Fillmore
Major Theme: Spirituality and abundance

In this book, Prosperity, Charles Fillmore walks you through a spiritual journey that shows you how faith can deliver you the life that you want to be leading.

Fillmore, another New Thought proponent, discusses the faith in the invisible substance and how God has provided abundance in each and every home.

He covers how keeping faith can help you feel more fulfilled and want less materialist possessions, leading to a greater sense of achievement in life and less desire for the common goods that so many people are chasing after.

This book will help to bring out your spiritual side and help you have faith in knowing that your future is well taken care of.

Psycho-Cybernetics (1960)

Maxwell Maltz
Major Theme: Self-Improvement and Self-Image

In Psycho-Cybernetics Maxwell Maltz is going to show you that you have the power to create the life that you want to be leading by shifting your viewpoint of yourself as well as others around you.

He goes into details about how your self-image is the key to leading a better life and how you can gain clarity and determination through imagery of what it is that you hope to achieve. In addition to that, he also goes into details of how you can use rational thinking to help bring better focus into your life and how to allow yourself to relax and let your natural tendencies work for you rather than against you.

Maltz was a highly successful plastic surgeon and he uses his experiences in that role to clearly illustrate the power of how we see ourselves as being a main determinant in whether we succeed or not.

Finally, he also shows you how you can turn a crisis situation around and make it work in a positive manner to help bring you to a state of higher health and happiness.

Science Of Mind (1938)

Ernest Holmes
Major Theme: Mental Enrichment and Power

In Science Of Mind, Ernest Holmes discusses how the mind works in many different ways, allowing you to gain insight and clarity into many of the events and occurrences that shape your existence.

He looks at what we consider to be 'man' and what we consider to be 'God' and how your spirit will guide you through life, impacting everything that you do.

In the second section of the book he talks about how the power of thought can completely change your life, turning around negative circumstances and allowing you to see clearly and how to make the most of the circumstances, moving forward to create the life that you desire.

He provides an overview of how to use prayer as a form of treatment during the difficult times and talks about faith and how this can keep you strong during times of difficulty.

Secret Of The Ages (1926)

Robert Collier
Major Theme: Self-Empowerment

Robert Collier was first known and best known in the early 20th Century as a highly successful direct mail copywriter. The *Robert Collier Letter Book*, which includes examples of some of Collier's best sales letters, is still in print and a valuable resource to modern day copywriters.

After being struck with a very serious illness, Collier began to read and study extensively about the power of the mind, especially its power to heal the body. After overcoming his illness Collier's attention turned to writing books that focused on the power of thought and mind.

In this book, he takes you through a journey that will give you a strong sense of self-empowerment as you realize that you are the master of your own universe. He teaches you that you are the one and only person who is responsible for your happiness and it is the day-to-day choices and decisions that you make that shape the life that you choose to lead.

If you don't currently like where you are in life, you have the power to change that. Through your inner being, you can alter the way you react to any given circumstance, learning to alter the way you view its impacts on you and learn from every setback that you face.

He teaches you the mental outlook that you need to be adopting if you want to achieve a life of fulfillment and happiness so you know exactly what to do in order to get to where you want to be.

Secret of the Ages was originally published in seven different small leather-bound editions. I presume the seven editions were released over time in a serial version which was a very popular way of selling books in those days. I once gifted one of my mentors, Bob Proctor, an autographed set of the originals and loved them so much myself I had to go get a set for my library.

See You At The Top (1975)

Zig Ziglar
Major Theme: Self-Improvement

This was either the second or third personal development book I read as a young twenty-something. When I first bought it the book was actually titled *Fleas, Biscuits and Pump Handles*. I'm not sure who made the decision to change it to *See You At The Top*, but that's a much more appropriate title for a very powerful book.

Zig covers all the main areas where you could benefit from some key self-improvement strategies to lead a healthier and more fulfilling lifestyle. It's important to realize that self-improvement doesn't come from just one area of your life and rather, a number of areas must align for best results.

Like all of his works, this book talks about adopting the right type of attitude that will bring about results. This was my first exposure to how "stinkin' thinkin'" can destroy your life. Zig also teaches how desire can play a role in the decisions that you make on a day-to-day basis, why goal setting is critical to success, how to form a healthier self-image, and how to foster the strongest relationships with others.

Perhaps the biggest impact this book had on my life was first learning that "you can have anything you want in life if you help enough other people get what they want." Incredible wisdom that has shaped my thoughts and actions ever since those days long ago when I first read those words.

Seeds Of Greatness (1983)

Denis Waitley
Major Theme: Self-Improvement and Self-Esteem

I believe Denis Waitley is the most effective author I know of when it comes to communicating ideas that will improve your self-esteem. After I had a chance to meet and get to know Denis he told me that he first wrote about these topics to help HIMSELF, when he was going through some challenging times in his life.

Seeds of Greatness is a book that is going to have you evaluating how you view yourself and the life that you've created and then take actionable steps to improve what you're thinking about yourself so that you can achieve what it is you desire.

The book is going to walk you through discussions on how to formulate a strong feeling of self-love which will then translate to greater feelings of self-worth and how you can release your natural creative energy to get more accomplished in everything that you do. You'll also learn how to harness the power of goal setting, the best way to foster stronger interpersonal relationships, as well as the power that self-beliefs can have over you.

For many years I carried extra copies of this book in my trunk so that when I met someone who was suffering from low self-esteem I could give them a personal copy. If you have any doubts about whether you deserve to be successful, if your self worth isn't what it should be, then put this on your short list of books to read.

Self Help (1859)

Samuel Smiles
Major Theme: Self-Improvement

This is one of the oldest books on the list, published in the middle of the 19th century. It's a little more difficult to read than modern day books but well worth the effort.

Smiles talks about learning your own personal strengths so that you can use them to your advantage, how to stop stressing out over the mundane events of everyday life, how to bust through a rut and other hard times, as well as how to be true to yourself and gain a higher level of self-respect.

This book will also walk you through a series of steps that you can take if you want to get further help beyond what is mentioned in the body and show you how to make sure that you're living every moment to the fullest in your everyday life.

Self Mastery Through Conscious Autosuggestion (1922)

Emile Coue
Major Theme: Autosuggestion

This was a hugely popular book in the 1920's and Coue, a French Psychologist, had a huge following as a result of it. In this book he offers a number of suggestions that are both practical and applicable to your real life world that you can put to use immediately to improve your day-to-day living and become the person you want to be.

His central theme is about the power of autosuggestion which others, like Napoleon Hill in *Think and Grow Rich,* also thought was an important part of succeeding.

Coue goes into discussions regarding both the conscious self as well as the unconscious self and how these interact to shape the world around you. In addition to this, he's also going to provide clues as to why you may be where you are today and what you can do moving forward to change that so that you can lead the happier life that you desire.

One of the main autosuggestions he is famous for, "Every day, in every way, I'm getting better and better", is still utilized by many.

Self-Reliance (1841)

Ralph Waldo Emerson
Major Theme: Self-change and improvement

Like Samuel Smiles' *Self Help*, this book is from the mid-19th century. And it's really not a book but a collection of essays that Emerson wrote to teach you the concept of self-reliance and what it means to lead a full and happy life. The essays remain popular because they are inspirational and motivational and will encourage you to take charge of your own life.

For anyone looking for a good read that will soothe their spirit and mind, it's a perfect book to check out.

7 Strategies For Wealth & Happiness (1985)

Jim Rohn
Major Theme: Achieving personal success

In this book on creating lasting change within yourself, Jim Rohn outlines that success is not dependent on either wealth or happiness, but rather the two go hand in hand and are both perfectly achievable with the right frame of mind.

This is a classic Rohn book that is concise and clear about the simple universal principles that he so eloquently wrote, spoke and taught in his legendary career.

Success! The Glenn Bland Method (1983)

Glenn Bland
Major Theme: Goal setting and self-improvement

If you've ever felt that you 'can't', this book is for you. Glenn Bland is going to illustrate to you how to achieve a higher level of self-confidence and belief in your ability to change your life and accomplish all that you have set out to do.

Far too many people never go after their goals simply because they don't believe that they will ever come to obtain them and this is what prevents them from even trying.

Using the techniques and strategies outlined in this book, you can finally get yourself putting forth the effort that you need to be in order to live the life that you've always dreamed of. Not a very well-known book but a personal development classic in every way!

The 21 Irrefutable Laws Of Leadership (1998)

John Maxwell
Major Theme: Leadership and social relationships

John Maxwell is a prolific writer and has written a number of international best-sellers. In my opinion this is one of his two or three best books and very definitely the very best leadership book period.

For anyone who is involved in a leadership position or who simply wants to learn how to manage people better, this book will help you do so. Maxwell discusses a number of leadership stories to give you inspiration for your own life and allows you to look inside yourself to find traits that you can develop to become a more effective leader.

This book will also provide you with exercises that you can use as you go through it to help pinpoint further areas you need to work on that will help improve your skills and communication abilities.

Finally, you'll learn how to influence people and command respect.

The 7 Habits Of Highly Effective People (1989)

Stephen Covey
Major Theme: Self-Improvement and Success

From its debut this has been near the top of business best-sellers and remains as popular today as it was more than twenty years ago. Covey goes over seven different habits that are characteristic among all of those who achieve great success in both their personal and career lives. The book talks about having the proper mindset that breeds success and how you can best go about your interactions with others to achieve the end results you desire.

This is very simple and straightforward teaching as Covey is known for. Full of practical ways to implement the 7 Habits, you'll pick this book up many times over the years.

The 80/20 Principle: The Secret To Achieving More With Less (1998)

Richard Koch
Major Theme: Productivity and self-improvement

Pareto's principle, also known as the 80-20 rule, was identified more than 100 years ago. In this book, Richard Koch breaks that principle down and how to use it to bring about rapid and long-lasting change in your life. He demonstrates how only 20% of what we do and where we spend our time is responsible for 80% of our results. On the other hand, 80% of our time is wasted or non-productive.

Reading this book will help you learn to focus your efforts on the 20% while eliminating those activities in the 80%.

This book will help you put into perspective how much what you do on a day-to-day basis really matters in the grand scheme of things and help you turn your focus to more important areas of your life. A very good read and once you understand Pareto's principle you can apply it in many ways. For instance, 20% of your customers produce 80% of your revenue. Better to focus on those 20% than on the 80%.

The Aladdin Factor (1995)

Mark Victor Hansen and Jack Canfield
Major Theme: Self-Improvement and accomplishment

The premise of this book is that one of the biggest reasons few of us ever attain the success that we desire is simply because we don't ask for what we want. We keep our deepest desires hidden, thinking that making requests that would move us closer to our goals are unreasonable and will not be perceived well by others.

In this book the authors teach you how to identify what it is that you want and what the power of asking can do. If you stop and think about it logically, the more you ask for what you want, the more your desire is cast out into the Universe where someone else may resonate with your request.

The Autobiography Of Andrew Carnegie And The Gospel Of Wealth (1889)

Andrew Carnegie
Major Theme: Inspirational/Autobiography

In this autobiography, Andrew Carnegie offers inspiration and motivation to anyone who wants to positively change their life, fostering a higher level of success, happiness, and self-fulfillment.

I enjoyed the book immensely because he goes into great detail about his life beginning with his earliest memories as a child. He chronicles all the choices that he made from a very early age right up until he became one of the richest people in the world. He talks about the influence that his parents and peers had on him and other forces that came to shape who he became later on in life.

Lots of great success lessons to be learned from this book. For anyone who enjoys reading autobiographies and wants a little extra inspiration for achievement in their own lives, this will be a must-read.

The Common Denominator Of Success (1940)

Albert E.N. Gray
Major Theme: Self-Improvement and success
In this book Albert Gray looks at what makes successful people successful. He assesses the common traits that those who are most successful often possess so that you can compare to your own characteristics and decide what it is that you need to be working on in order to move forward and reach the goals that you have set for yourself.

Gray, who was an executive with Prudential Life Insurance company, first delivered the message as a major address to the 1940 NALU (National Association of Life Underwriters) annual convention in Philadelphia.

The premise behind this book is that your success is shaped and influenced by each and every decision that you make on a day-to-day basis and only by making the right, results-producing decisions will you move towards the path that you hope to.

This book is both inspirational and encouraging and is a very quick read.

The Dynamic Laws Of Prosperity (1962)

Catherine Ponder
Major Theme: Abundance thinking

In *The Dynamic Laws Of Prosperity* Catherine Ponder reveals all the many secrets that she's learned over the course of her life that drive love, wealth, happiness, and success.

She is a minister of the non-denominational Unity faith and has been described as "the Norman Vincent Peale among lady ministers." So her writings naturally carry a very strong spiritual slant.

Anyone who has ever felt stuck in a rut will definitely appreciate what this book will do for their mindset.

The Edinburgh And Dore Lectures On Mental Science (1904)

Thomas Troward
Major Theme: Science of mind

I heard Bob Proctor teaching on this book one night on a tele-seminar years ago when I was a member of his mentoring program. It is based around a series of lectures that were given regarding the connection between the mind and the world we create around us.

Troward was a judge and highly educated so his writing is more formal than most. It was a little more difficult to read but his way of describing important principles has a big impact on your present thinking. Many well-known figures of the New Thought movement like

Emmet Fox, Ernest Holmes and Joseph Murphy were greatly influenced by Troward.

Throughout the book you'll learn about the body, soul, and spirit and how the mind plays a critical part in the development of each of these elements.

The Five Love Languages (1992)

Gary Chapman
Major Theme: Romantic relationship improvement

This is one of the very best "relationship books" I've ever read. It covers what happens to love after the wedding takes place and what you can be doing to help improve your connection, deepening your love for each other as time goes on.

This book also offers advice on everyday things that you can do with your partner to help keep your bond strong and reduce the risk that life moves you in different directions.

You will immediately grasp the whole idea behind this book when you identify your love language as well as your partner's, and it will give you a new perspective of your relationship. Chapman finishes the book by talking about the fact that loving is a choice and how you can sustain love through difficult times.

The Game Of Life And How To Play It (1925)

Florence Scovel Shinn
Major Theme: Self-Improvement

This book is a quick and simple read that offers some great insights into spiritual laws of the universe. Her writing is simple and direct and has been popular over the years with Unity church members.

While reading this book you'll come to gain a deeper sense of meaning for both your own life as well as the role you play in others and come away feeling a greater sense of being fulfilled and living on purpose.

The book leaves you with a set of affirmations that you can use on a daily basis that will help to keep you in a more positive frame of mind and feeling great about yourself and the direction that you're headed.

The Go Getter (1921)

Peter Kyne
Major Theme: Inspirational and self-development

This book will surprise you!

First of all, you'll probably read it in one sitting because it's a very short book but mostly because you'll get caught up in a great story.

The Go Getter re-enforces the fact that far too many people just sit around and let life happen to them, hoping that it works out for the best in the end. In reality though, the only person who is responsible for your own happiness is yourself, so without the tenacity to go after what it is you desire, the chances of attaining this happiness will be slim.

Persistence is the one trait that I've seen in every successful person I've ever known or ever studied. And this book will give you some new lessons in persistence that will cause you to chuckle. This is a fun, fast read!

The Greatest Salesman In The World (1968)

Og Mandino
Major Theme: Sales techniques and persuasion

Recently my daughter told me that her significant other was starting in a sales job and wondered what I would recommend to help him. After thinking about it a bit I flashed back to my early twenties and the impact this little book of Og's had on me

Whether you're in a sales position or not, this book will help you learn the top habits you need to develop to help you "close the deal." This book will provide insights into persuasion and what it takes to understand the person you are selling to, tapping into their innermost desires, wants, and needs.

You'll love the story of Hafid, a poor camel boy who achieves a life of abundance. The "Ten Scrolls" had a lifetime impact on me and continues to play a big role in my success. And I want to reiterate that this book is not just for sales people. Actor Matthew McConaughey cited this book as having changed his life and has given away many copies of it.

The Law Of Success In 16 Lessons (1928)

Napoleon Hill
Major Theme: Success and self-mastery

Most people know of Napoleon Hill because of his multi-million best-selling *Think and Grow Rich.* But what most people don't know is that *Think and Grow Rich* is in many ways just a summary of his more mammoth work, *The Law of Success in 16 Lessons*, an all-encompassing encyclopaedia of success that is more than 1,100 pages.

Many people know that Hill met Andrew Carnegie when he was a young reporter and received a commission (unpaid) to write a book about the philosophy of success. Carnegie introduced Hill to the great financial successes of the day like Firestone, Ford, Edison and hundreds of others.

Over the course of twenty years Hill interviewed and studied these successful people and analyzed the characteristics that helped them succeed. The *Law of Success* is the fruit of that work and is a must read for any serious student of success.

The Magic Of Believing (1948)

Claude Bristol
Major Theme: Self-belief and control

This book was my first real study of just the power of belief. It was a great introduction and insight about how powerful your belief is in the results you see in your life. In my case it was the last piece of the puzzle for me. Once I got my self-belief going I started rockin' and rollin'.

Many people are fast to let their environment shape

who they become, but the point of this book is to teach you that it doesn't have to be this way. It will provide a series of mental experiments you can go through that will illustrate how you currently are viewing your life and the power you have so that you can begin to make the necessary changes that are required to get you to where you want to be.

The legendary comedienne Phyllis Diller and entertainer Liberace both credit this book for lifting them from mediocrity to huge success.

The Magic Of Thinking Big (1959)

David Schwartz
Major Theme: Self-Development and achievement

In many ways this will always be my number one personal development book. For sure it was my first one. I don't remember how I came across the book but I still have that first book I read in my early twenties.

I tell people that I was young enough and dumb enough to believe what I read and to act on it. Within six months of reading it I was buying my first business even though the only thing I owned at the time was a car payment.

I've read it over and over in the last 35 years and it still amazes me how powerful this writing is. One line from the book literally changed my life, but I didn't remember it from the book. I heard a speaker quote it from stage: "The size of your success is determined by the size of your belief."

When I heard those words uttered it hit me like a ton of bricks and I went to work over the next ninety days, working harder than I've ever worked in my life, on strengthening my belief. My life hasn't been the same since.

No matter what else you do with the information you get from this book, I hope you will stop right now and go buy an eBook or paperback, even a used book if you must, of *The Magic of Thinking Big.*

The Magic Story (1900)

Frederic Van Rensselaer Day
Major Theme: Inspiration and success

This book, which is over 100 years old, is a classic read for anyone who is looking for a little motivation and inspiration to achieve greatness in their own life. It offers a number of wise pieces of advice that you'll find applicable to your own situation and that will help you achieve your own personal goals.

Don't be fooled by the short page count of this book – while it may not have many pages, the pages it contains will really make a difference in your life and you'll enjoy the "story."

The Majesty Of Calmness (1898)

William George Jordan
Major Theme: Practicing self-control

This book takes a look at the impact of our current daily

lives on the level of happiness that we're achieving. The premise of the book is that far too many of us are rapidly rushing off to our many obligations without taking time to really enjoy life and all that it offers.

The book touches upon the power of personal influence and self-reliance and allows you to look at failure in a different light and see it as a stepping-stone to greatness.

Even though it was written well over 100 years ago this book can be a tremendous help in the times we currently live.

The Master Key System (1912)

Charles F. Haanel
Major Theme: Mind/Success development

The Master Key System is all about forming the correct frame of mind and thinking pattern to yield maximum success in your day-to-day life. In this book, Haanel will go over the basics of the mind, helping you gain a firmer understanding of how the mind works and influences the events that shape your own life.

In addition to this he speaks about realizing the mental resources that you have available to you and freeing your mind to the most creative state it can be in.

For those who enjoy introspection and learning about their own self-power and capabilities, this will definitely be a book you'll want to take in. Napoleon Hill, the author of *Think and Grow Rich* is said to have been greatly influenced by this book.

The Mastery Of Destiny (1909)

James Allen
Major Theme: Personal Development

After I had begun giving away eBook copies of *As A Man Thinketh*, I found a number of other Allen books and this is one of the best ones. Like all of his books it was written to teach you how to gain control over your mind and build the future that you are looking for. He goes over the concept of self-control and what it means to your day-to-day living as well as how you can improve your concentration level and remain focused regardless of what task you happen to be working on.

He also outlines how getting involved in meditation can bring you to a place of health and well-being and the power of living on purpose. This is more of the classic style that Allen has and may be a bit deeper than *As A Man Thinketh.*

The Message Of A Master (1929)

John McDonald
Major Theme: Personal Growth And Development

This is not a very well known book and I just happened to bump into several mentions of it on the web. When I read it the first time I was mesmerized. The first half of the book is an interesting story that pulls you into the ultimate message of this book.

The second half of the book then breaks down the messages of the story and how to implement those principles into your life. This is a quick read but it is very much focused on a handful of principles that ensure success.

The Millionaire Next Door (1996)

Thomas Stanley
Major Theme: Wealth development and strategy

Hollywood and the media have given us an image of what wealth represents and what wealthy people act like and "look like." Dr. Stanley blows that image to smithereens with his famous study that resulted in *The Millionaire Next Door.*

Stanley shares a number of true stories of how the 'guy and gal next door' achieved financial success and the personality traits that allowed them to do so. And they're the "salt of the earth" type traits and principles that have always created success.

This book inspires and motivates you to THINK when it comes to wealth building.

The Miracle Of Right Thought (1910)

Orison Swett Marden
Major Theme: Personal Development

In many ways this is a larger and expanded version of James Allen's classic *As A Man Thinketh.* It talks about the power of thought and how it can shape and influence the person that you come to be.

Each and every day you are creating the existence around you and this book helps you see that you do have the power to control your destiny. It outlines how you can use the power of thought and the way you perceive your daily events to breed a happier and healthier life that is filled with joy and success.

There are several books by Marden included in this book but he wrote many more that could qualify. I personally love his writing and I know many others who share my beliefs about Marden's work. This is my favorite of Marden's books but you'll benefit from any that have his name on them.

The One Minute Manager (1981)

Ken Blanchard
Major Theme: People Management and leadership

In this book, Ken Blanchard discusses what it takes to make a good manager and what you must do to achieve success when managing a group situation.

He talks about simple everyday strategies that will only take one minute to start implementing that will produce noticeable differences in productivity, achievement, as well as team unity. These include one-minute goals, one-minute praisings, and one-minute reprimands. You'll learn what each of these means and how to use them in your own specific scenario.

This book is a great read for anyone in a management position or who is in a leadership role. I had no formal management training and found myself in a position with more than twenty employees when I came across this book. It was an easy-to-understand strategy and one that I know produced positive benefits.

The Power Of Concentration (1918)

Theron Q. Dumont
Major Theme: Mental and personal development

This book is going to teach you how great the power of the mind can be and how you can use its powers to harness the life that you want to lead. You'll get an inside glimpse into how concentration can assist with career success, personal success, as well as financial success, and learn strategies that you can start using immediately to improve your own concentration levels.

This book talks about how concentration can bring you to a higher level of being and how to use it to capitalize all the resources you have available to you in the effort to meet your long-term goals.

The Power Of Positive Thinking (1952)

Norman Vincent Peale
Major Theme: Personal Development

I like Zig Ziglar's quote about the idea of positive thinking: "Positive thinking won't let you do anything, but it will let you do everything better than negative thinking will." And in my opinion no one writes about the power of positive thinking better than Peale does.

You'll learn how your current frame of mind is shaping

the reality that you call your existence and what you can do to enhance this frame of mind to breed higher levels of success and happiness. Peale, who was a long-time and popular minister in New York, also writes about how faith comes into play to keep you going during the difficult times.

If you feel like you need a complete change of pace and a new frame of mind, this book will help to provide it. And I can tell you from experience, if things are going generally negative in your life right now, this book is like a life raft!

The Power Of Your Subconscious Mind (1963)

Joseph Murphy
Major Theme: Mental development

The primary purpose of this book is to get you digging deeper into your subconscious mind so that you can learn how it's driving your decisions on a daily basis, shaping your own reality.

Many of us make choices and decisions in our everyday life automatically without thought and this book gets you looking at those choices and assessing whether they are working for you or against you with the goals that you have set.

After reading this book you'll have greater insight into why some of the events and predicaments of your life are the way they are and what you may be able to do to change that moving forward.

You'll gain practical tips and techniques to use immediately in all areas of your life. The book does have a strong spiritual slant because Murphy was an ordained minister, so much of what you learn about your subconscious is as much spirit as science.

The Purpose Driven Life (2002)

Rick Warren
Major Theme: Self-growth and spirituality

If you feel as though you need a sense of purpose and direction in your life, Warren's best-seller is a great book to invest in.

Warren, another ordained minister with a huge following, outlines God's master plan for your life and how you can be all that you can be as you move through the years. You'll be taken through a 40-day spiritual journey that will help you answer important questions you have about your life and realize where you want to and should be going with it.

You'll gain a deeper understanding for humanity and help to see your life in a new light that you've never considered before.

For anyone looking for a spiritual journey and transformation, this book will help provide it.

The Richest Man In Babylon (1926)

George Clason
Major Theme: Financial principles

In this book, George Clason shares the personal story of one of the most financially successful men of his time and offers inspiration to all those who seek out greater levels of wealth.

Throughout the book you'll learn what it takes to accumulate larger sums of wealth and how to control your spending urges during times when you need to be saving.

You'll gain insight into what it means to become wealthy and how through determination and careful planning, achieving financial success is possible. Many people consider this to be the classic book for instilling sound financial principles and it continues to be a best-seller.

The Road Less Traveled (1978)

M. Scott Peck
Major Theme: Personal growth and problem solving

In this book, psychiatrist Dr. Scott Peck looks at what you should be doing in order to overcome the problems in your life and create the changes that you desire.

He recognizes the fact that far too many people shy away from their problems due to the fact that they are too painful to face and offers insight into the ways that you can overcome your fears and tackle what will help to enhance your life in the long term.

This book will help bring you to a higher understanding of yourself and what it means to lead in a healthy and fulfilled manner, so is a good read for anyone looking for some self-improvement. I personally favor this book for any time in your life when it seems all the wheels have come off your wagon and nothing's going right.

The Science Of Being Great (1911)

Wallace Wattles
Major Theme: Personal Development

The next two books are by a somewhat enigmatic writer of the early twentieth century. His best known book is *The Science of Getting Rich*, which achieved its biggest exposure after it was featured in the blockbuster DVD, *The Secret.*

The Science of Being Great is really a companion book for SGR, with this book focusing more on developing your self and especially your self-esteem.

The Science Of Getting Rich (1910)

Wallace Wattles
Major Theme: Financial Development

My first exposure came via a program that Bob Proctor did about this book. That program, likewise called the Science of Getting Rich, radically altered my thinking about creating wealth. The program included a word-for-word study guide of the book that Bob taught from, so I have literally taken apart every single word of this book and powerful words they are.

These concepts are apt to be foreign to most upon their first reading and that's why the impact on your results can be so big. These are truly universal principles that do have the power to move mountains.

Like *As A Man Thinketh*, and many of the other great reads on this list, this is not a very large book. So be sure to include it on your early must-read list. It will shape a lot of your thinking after that.

The Science Of The Mind (1938)

Ernest Holmes
Major Theme: Mental and personal development

In this book you'll be guided through information about how the mind works and the role it plays in shaping the reality that you see today. You'll learn how to best use your mind to achieve greatness and how to better balance your mind, spirit, soul, and body.

Holmes was a New Thought minister and founder of a Spiritual movement known as Religious Science so all of his writings have a strong spiritual focus. You'll learn the influence that spirituality plays in your day-to-day existence and how to maintain a sense of self while still carrying out your role in God's world.

You'll also gain insight into the power of prayer as well as how faith can help you through trying times.

The Seven Spiritual Laws of Success (1994)

Deepak Chopra
Major Theme: Spirituality and self-growth

Spiritual and motivational speaker Deepak Chopra discusses his seven laws of spirituality in this book that will get you thinking about the way that you're living and changes that you could be making to foster a greater existence.

The laws that he'll teach you about include the law of potentiality, the law of giving, the law of karma, the law of least effort, the law of intention and desire, the law of detachment, as well as the Law of Dharma (purpose in life).

At this point in this book you may be questioning why so many of the books have spiritual messages. As Bob Proctor explained to me and others: "We are not bodies with a spirit but spirits with a body." So if we overlook our spirit we cannot truly become the person we were created to be.

I have made it a point not to let someone's dogma get in the way of me learning all I can about how the spirit functions and how to grow my spiritual life. That's why I can easily read Rick Warren (an evangelical Christian minister) or Deepak Chopra (Eastern Spiritual philosopher). And I would encourage you to develop the same practice in your reading.

The Strangest Secret (1956)

Earl Nightingale
Major Theme: Personal Growth and development

The Strangest Secret was a record in the beginning. That's right, one of those round black platters with a hole in the middle of it. In just a few years after its introduction it became the first spoken word album to win a Gold Record with more than one million sold.

The message became so successful that it literally ushered in the modern day personal development industry. Since then the famous audio recording has been converted to a small book (and eBook) and in the written word it may be even more powerful than in the spoken word.

Earl Nightingale talks about a secret that he discovered in his own world that lead to the opening of doors that he never thought possible and a brand new way of living that would foster greater wealth, success, and happiness.

He calls it the "strangest secret" and it's the six most powerful words on the planet, "you become what you think about." Put this on your early must-read list!

The Success System That Never Fails (1962)

W. Clement Stone
Major Theme: Success and personal achievement

This is another of these classic books that I first read in my twenties. At the time Stone had taken over Success Magazine and turned it around as well as hiring and partnering with *Think and Grow Rich* author Napoleon Hill. Stone had made his billions in the insurance business and was at the stage of his life where he was giving back that knowledge.

The Success System That Never Fails is a book that's designed to help you learn what it takes to achieve success and greatness along with all the steps that you'll take to get there. The book outlines how to prepare yourself for success through key actions that you take today and how you can be a self-builder, creating your own level of success. Stone includes a lot of lessons he learned along his path from an impoverished child who went to work at six to help support his mother to becoming one of the wealthiest people in the world. A true Horatio Alger story.

The Ultimate Gift (2001)

Jim Stovall
Major Theme: Appreciation and self-growth

The Ultimate Gift is a great book for anyone who could benefit from more gratitude in their everyday life (which is about all of us) and who needs to gain appreciation for all that life has to offer. It is a very entertaining story that will pull you into a great plot with a surprise ending.

It was written by Jim Stovall who I had the good fortune to feature as a keynote speaker at one of our events a few years ago. Jim was a promising young athlete when he began to lose his sight, ultimately becoming totally blind. The way he handled that obstacle is a tremendous inspiration in and of itself, and it very definitely has had an impact on all of Jim's writings.

The University Of Success (1982)

Og Mandino
Major Theme: Self-achievement and success

This five-hundred plus page book is a complete "education" in success broken up into ten semesters of five lessons each. These 50 lessons are taught by a "faculty" of some of the biggest names in personal development including James Allen, Napoleon Hill, Dr. Maxwell Maltz, Dale Carnegie and others. My personal copy has underlined wisdom on almost every page.

Each lesson stands alone so you can read one lesson and reflect upon it and act upon it before moving on to the next one. I was amazed at the change in my thinking from EVERY lesson—they were that powerful!

The book will also teach you how to improve your self-esteem and motivation and to eliminate bad habits from your life that are only holding you back from reaching your goals.

All in all, you'll truly have an education after you finish at this "university!"

The Will To Believe (1896)

William James
Major Theme: Personal growth

Once you begin an in-depth study of personal development you'll see William James' name everywhere. He was a well-known psychologist and philosopher of the late 19th and early 20th centuries.

One of my most favorite quotes comes from James, "The greatest discovery of my generation is that a human being can alter his life by altering his attitudes." That was a real eye-opener to me when I first read it.

This was actually a lecture that James gave before it became a popular book.

In it you'll be guided through your own personal journey as you recollect your past experiences and look at what you want for the future. You'll gain insight and clarity on the life that you're living and where you're headed.

Maybe for the first time you'll be testing your own thoughts and beliefs that are taking you on your great self-growth journey.

Think And Grow Rich (1937)

Napoleon Hill
Major Theme: Financial advice and development

No one seems to know for sure but perhaps as many as 100 hundred million copies of this book have been sold since Hill introduced it during the depression days of 1937. Many people believe it to be the greatest personal growth book of all time and I'd certainly put it in the top five.

Think And Grow Rich shows you money-making secrets that will forever change your life. But more than just about making money, these are really universal and sound secrets of success in any endeavor, regardless of how much money may be involved. After reading this book you'll have a new viewpoint on what it means to become successful and how to go about doing so in your own personal life.

You'll learn concepts that you've never considered

regarding money before and see precisely what it takes to become wealthy. And not some pie-in-the-sky theories. These are the EXACT principles used by five hundred of the most financially successful Americans ever.

There have been a number of revised editions released in later years but I personally prefer the original 1937 edition. **You can get a FREE print copy of the original edition here www.Get-My-Free-Book.net**

Think Like A Winner! (1991)

Walter Doyle Staples
Major Theme: Personal Success

Think Like A Winner! Is a great book about human behavior and personal potential. This book will discuss what makes people successful and the influences that can shape who you become. You'll also take a look at the role of human behavior in whether or not you see the level of success you're after and also how the mind works to create the you that you are.

I'd never heard of Dr. Staples before I bought this book and haven't heard a whole lot about him since, but this is one of those "sleeper" books that will surprise you.

Thoughts Are Things (1889)

Prentice Mulford
Major Theme: Mental growth and development

This book will lead you through mental growth and development as you consider the material mind versus the spiritual mind. You will assess your current viewpoints and experiences and discover how those are shaping the reality in which you live.

You'll then discover how to transform your mind so that you can think about events in a new light, encouraging a higher overall level of personal growth and development.

Three Magic Words: The Key To Power, Peace, And Plenty (1972)

U.S. Anderson
Major Theme: Success and achievement

For anyone who is looking for a greater overall level of success and achievement in their life, this book can help to offer that. It will outline for you the three keys to living a successful life including power, peace, and plenty.

You'll learn how to turn the natural power that you possess into a greater level of success in your life while you achieve all that you set out to.

As is true of all of Anderson's writings, you'll also discover how God drives everything that you do and take steps to answer your own personal problems and create a happier and healthier existence.

Tough Times Never Last But Tough People Do (1983)

Robert H. Schuller
Major Theme: Personal Development

This is one of those books that comes along at just the

right time in your life and things are never the same again after you read it. I was undergoing some particularly "tough times" when I read this book and boy did its message hit me right between the eyes.

If I've given away one copy of this book, I've given away a hundred—to friends (and even strangers) who, like me, had hit a rough patch. Dr. Schuller is a long-time Christian minister so the book has a decidedly Christian spiritual tone, but I've given it to my Hebrew (and even agnostic) friends who have raved about its wisdom.

It will provide you with the foundational knowledge of why some people can endure hard times with a positive mindset and attitude while others cannot. You'll learn how to take charge of your own life, making changes that will make you more tenacious and better able to cope with anything that comes your way.

Unstoppable (1998)

Cynthia Kersey
Major Theme: Inspiration and motivation

Bob Proctor sent me this book in '98 or '99 and it's always been one of my favorites because of all of the incredible stories of regular people who became unstoppable in their quest for success. In a few minutes every morning you can read one story and I promise it will change the way you start your day. It'll make you UNSTOPPABLE!

I've also had the great privilege to become great friends with Cynthia and she's appeared on our stage in the past. She is a great example (and great teacher) of how to excel despite being faced with huge obstacles.

Great reading!

Wake Up And Live (1936)

Dorothea Brande
Major Theme: Personal growth and development

I first heard about Dorothea and her book when I was listening to Earl Nightingale in *The Strangest Secret*. Like a lot of the great classics it's a quick read that doesn't beat around the bush but gets to the point. You'll learn what it means to fail and how you can use your own personal failures to fuel your desire for growth and personal discovery. A tremendous lesson for most people who don't succeed because they're afraid to fail.

This book will highlight what you can start doing today to create a life that is without stress and that brings you a higher sense of enjoyment and feelings of accomplishment. You'll get the answers to the questions of why you react in certain ways as you do and help gain insight into how you can improve yourself so that you are better equipped to handle trying situations down the road.

Walden (1854)

Henry David Thoreau
Major Theme: Autobiography/Inspiration

Thoreau wrote my most favorite success quote ever, "If one advances confidently in the direction of his dreams, and endeavors to live the life which he has imagined, he will meet with success unexpected in common hours."

For a time in my life I taped that quote to everything—my computer, my bathroom mirror, the dashboard in my car, etc. At that time I was hoping it was true and hoping that my constant affirmation of it would make it come true. One day it dawned on me that I could honestly say that I had fully realized the promise of that quote because I had achieved "success unexpected in common hours." It was a humbling feeling!

In this book, Thoreau recollects his journey through life and all the many events that he survived and the meaning of it all. It is a bit difficult to read because Thoreau is a very complex writer, but persist, this message is worth it!

What To Say When You Talk To Yourself (1982)

Shad Helmstetter
Major Theme: Personal growth

In *What To Say When You Talk To Yourself,* you'll learn the power that your own pattern of thought and self-talk has on you. This whole concept was a huge aha to me and my life went to a different level after I fully implemented this principle and became very conscious of what I was telling myself every day.

You'll learn the importance of structuring your own self-talk in a way that breeds a higher level of success and well-being and how to get rid of poor thought patterns that hinder you from achieving greatness. Most people will very quickly realize why they haven't reached their potential and will recognize the poor "scripting" they've been engaged in.

This book is a "game-changer."

When Bad Things Happen To Good People (1981)

Harold Kushner
Major Theme: Self-Reflection and Improvement

Kushner is a very prominent American rabbi and his book is full of spiritual overtones and wisdom. And just as I've pointed out about some of the other authors in this book who write with Christian and New Thought influences, the message is really a non-denominational one. If you feel that you're down on your luck and that it seems as though life never goes your way, this book can help you gain some insight and give you hope for a better future.

Sometimes life can deal you a bad set of cards and the only thing you can do in these instances is play them the best way that you know how. This book is going to illustrate to you why bad things happen to good people and what you can do to overcome obstacles that stand in your way. Still a best-seller after more than 30 years and for good reason. Read it!

Who Moved My Cheese (1998)

Spencer Johnson
Major Theme: Self-growth

Almost everyone has a 'master plan' for how they would like their life to progress. Sadly though, few people ever achieve that exact plan. Life throws a curve ball at you and you're faced with obstacles that must be overcome.

If you feel as though your life has gone off-course and you just don't know what to do to get back on track, this book will provide some insight. You'll learn how to reframe your mind to a more positive thought pattern so that you can find yourself back on route to the path you set out to attain.

Another quick read and one you'll enjoy.

Wooden: A Lifetime Of Observations And Reflections On And Off The Court (1997)

John Wooden
Major Theme: Inspiration/Autobiography

No coach in the history of the game of basketball has come anywhere close to the record of John Wooden—an amazing 10 national collegiate basketball championships during 12 years at UCLA.

His wins came just as much as a result of the wisdom he imparted to his players as the X's and O's he drew on the board. Until he died just shy of his 100th birthday, Wooden continued to get a steady stream of visits and calls from his former players who revered him.

In this book he shares with you his journey through the wins and losses and how it shaped his character and that of his players. He looks at how families, values, and virtues influence your daily life decisions and how success, competition, and achievement will also influence an individual's growth and development.

This inspirational story makes for an excellent read by anyone involved in sport or competitive industries.

Working With The Law (1964)

Raymond Holliwell
Major Theme: Self-Growth

This is another book that Bob Proctor introduced me to. It is an incredibly insightful look into the various elements of life and the laws of nature. You'll get a glimpse into such laws as the law of forgiveness, the law of sacrifice, the law of obedience, the law of success, as well as the law of increase.

Throughout your journey reading this book you'll come to question many ways that you view your current life and start to see things in a new manner, hopefully fostering greater success and fulfillment.

You Can If You Think You Can (1974)

Norman Vincent Peale
Major Theme: Self-Esteem/belief

I've never read a Peale book that I didn't fall in love with. His writing is so engaging and so effective. *You Can If You Think You Can* is an excellent book for anyone who needs a self-esteem boost and is looking to achieve greatness in their life.

If you often feel overwhelmed by your shortcomings or let fear stop you from doing things in life that you wished you would do, this book can help you overcome that so that you can lead a more fulfilled existence.

Peale's spiritual influence (he was a very popular pastor) never offends and always enhances his message. Hard to pick my Peale favorite but this one comes awful close because of the emphasis on self-esteem, which I really had to work on.

You Were Born Rich (1997)

Bob Proctor
Major Theme: Financial success

One company owner thought so much of this book he ordered 30,000 copies to distribute to members of his organization! In great Bob Proctor style he walks you through a series of self-questions and reflections on where you are today and where you want to be going with regards to your financial wealth. He helps you see that success is not something you don't have but rather something that you have the power to create if you use the right strategy and take action.

He illustrates that success is already right before you and all you need to do is put the pieces of the puzzle together and you will start leading the life that you want to lead. If you've never been exposed to any of Bob's teachings this is a great place to start.

You'll See It When You Believe It: The Way To Your Personal Transformation (2001)

Wayne Dyer
Major Theme: Personal development

Wayne Dyer has other books that have been more popular than this one, but in my humble opinion this one influenced me a lot more. It's probably because he focuses on the power of belief and in my own life that was so critical to my ultimate success.

Dyer leads you through information about how your thoughts shape your reality and how to live a life that's full of abundance.

In addition to that you'll also learn what role detachment plays in your current state of being and help to discover how forgiveness is critical to optimal health and well-being.

You^2 (1997)

Price Pritchett
Major Theme: Personal and business success

You^2 (You squared) is yet another book that Bob Proctor introduced me to. Even though it's a mere 35-pages long I predict it will rock your life as much as it did mine and everybody else that I've ever recommended it to.

I carry this book with me in my computer bag so I can pull it out and read it when I'm feeling overwhelmed by some task. And I'm certainly going to read it before any visit with Bob because he's always going to ask me when was the last time I read it.

You'll learn how to quit trying harder and actually make the effort that you are putting in pay-off at a higher level. But more than anything, you'll really learn that it's not such a huge leap from where you're at to where you want to go. When you can see that from a new perspective you truly begin to believe things are possible which once seemed impossible.

Your Invisible Power (1921)

Genevieve Behrend
Major Theme: Personal development

In this book Genevieve Behrend walks you through information about how to harness your own natural powers and turn them into success and fulfillment in your life. She talks about the relationships between the mental and physical form of power and how to create a mental picture that will drive you in all that you do.

She talks about how to gain financial and interpersonal success in your life, while creating feelings of joy and wealth. This book will inspire you to create greatness with your life and leave you ready to take action to a new beginning.

Day by Day with James Allen (2003)

Vic Johnson
Major Theme: Daily Meditations on Personal development

OK, so this is not included in the 101 Best. This is actually the 102nd book that I'm listing. But since it's mine, I'm quite prejudiced about it. But frankly, it has a place in this book because my book is really a distillation of all the great books I've read. And in this one I quote extensively from many of the books here.

I'm very proud that this book has had a five-star rating at Amazon since its debut and that it's sold more than 75,000 copies. It's also been translated into Japanese, Czech, Slovak and Farsi (the Persian language of Iran).

But I'm most proud of another achievement with Day by Day. The book is a daily meditation on the words written by James Allen, author of the classic *As A Man Thinketh.* After the legendary Charlie "Tremendous" Jones read my book he sent me a letter telling me that it was the best interpretation of *As A Man Thinketh* that he's ever read! As they say in the MasterCard commercial: PRICELESS!

Now What?

You've been given the "keys to the kingdom." It's up to you now to use them to go open the doors of opportunity in your life. It's vitally important that you READ books – if not these then others that can facilitate your growth. As Mark Twain wrote, "The man who does not read good books has no advantage over the man who cannot read them."

But the mere reading of any books will not magically transport you to the success you desire. If it were true that all you had to do was read and you'd be successful, then the most successful people in the world would be librarians and professors.

Knowledge is not power as is commonly believed. Only knowledge ACTED UPON has power. In my case my commitment to reading became so voracious that I finally read enough books that the reading alone influenced me to ACTION. But most people don't want to read anywhere close to the two books a week I was averaging at one point. So the simpler course is simply to ACT on what you read AS YOU READ IT.

For instance, when you read something in a book that strikes you as life altering, stop right there. Don't read any further until you put that principle (or principles) into action in your life. Highlight it and underline it in the book. Write it on an index card and put it in your pocket or purse. Put it on a pop-up on your computer. Tape it to your mirror or the dash of your car. Do whatever you can do to keep it in front of you.

Then look for every opportunity to act on your new knowledge. You won't have to do this but a couple of times to be convinced of how powerful it is. And the transformation in your life will keep you committed to the practice!

I have a serious addiction. I'm not ashamed to admit it. In fact, I'm rather proud of it. I'm addicted to books! After I saw Bob Proctor's office in his home, where he's surrounded by thousands of books, I insisted during our lake house remodel that my office be designed where I would sit in the middle of all my books.

Like Bob, I have a special section for the books that other authors have signed to me. A section for collectibles, like an original (and autographed) 1937 version of *Think and Grow Rich*, and a section for my books that have been translated into other languages. Some days I just sit here in my haven of books, stare out at a postcard view of the lake we live on, and wonder in amazement what my life would have been like without all my "friends."

In 1994, at the event where I bought my first copy of *As A Man Thinketh,* I first heard Charlie "Tremendous" Jones utter his famous exhortation: "You're the same today as you'll be in five years except for two things; the books you read and the people you associate with."

On that day I made an unbreakable pledge to myself that I would make the most of those two principles, and as Robert Frost wrote in the *Road Not Taken*, "that has made all the difference." I know, too, that these books will make a difference in your life. I hope you will avail yourself of them.

For a free book of Napoleon Hill's classic *Think and Grow Rich*, go to www.Get-My-Free-Book.net

•••

Other Books from Laurenzana Press

The Strangest Secret by Earl Nightingale

Memory Improvement : How to Improve Your Memory in Just 30 Days by Ron White

Persistence & Perseverance: Dance Until It Rains by The Champions Club

The Law of Attraction: How To Get What You Want by Robert Collier

Time Management Tips: 101 Best Ways to Manage Your Time by Lucas McCain

Get Motivated: 101 Best Ways to Get Started, Keep Going and Finish Strong by Lucas McCain

Successful & Healthy Aging: 101 Best Ways to Feel Younger & Live Longer by Lisa J. Johnson

Self Confidence Secrets: How To Be Outgoing and Overcome Shyness by Lucas McCain

Happiness Habits: 21 Secrets to Living a Fun and Outrageously Rewarding Life by Lucas McCain

Self Help Books: The 101 Best Personal Development Classics by Vic Johnson

Overcoming Fear: 101 Best Ways to Overcome Fear and Anxiety and Take Control of Your Life Today! by Lucas McCain

Public Speaking Fear? 21 Secrets To Succeed In Front of Any Crowd by Lucas McCain

Going Green : 101 Ways To Save A Buck While You Save The Earth by Lucas McCain

Stress Management : 101 Best Ways to Relieve Stress and Really Live Life by Lucas McCain

Should I Divorce? 11 Questions To Answer Before You Decide to Stay or Go by Jennifer Jessica

Divorce Recovery: 101 Best Ways To Cope, Heal And Create A Fabulous Life After a Divorce by Jennifer Jessica

Should I Have a Baby? 10 Questions to Answer BEFORE You Get Pregnant by Jennifer Jessica

Stop Procrastinating: 101 Best Ways to Overcome Procrastination NOW! by Lucas McCain

Think and Grow Rich : The Lost Secret by Vic Johnson

Should I Get Married ? 10 Questions to Answer Before You Say I Do by Jennifer Jessica

Meditation Techniques: How To Meditate For Beginners And Beyond by Lucas McCain

Fast NLP Training: Persuasion Techniques To Easily Get What You Want by Lucas McCain

How To Attract a Woman: The Secret Handbook of What Women Want in a Man by Jennifer Jessica

Cure Anxiety Now! 21 Ways To Instantly Relieve Anxiety & Stop Panic Attacks by Lucas McCain

About The Author

Eleven years ago Vic Johnson was totally unknown in the personal development field. Since that time he's created six of the most popular personal development sites on the Internet. One of them, AsAManthinketh.net has given away over 400,000 copies of James Allen's classic book. Three of them are listed in the top 5% of websites in the world (English language).

This success has come despite the fact that he and his family were evicted from their home sixteen years ago and the next year his last automobile was repossessed. His story of redemption and victory has inspired thousands around the world as he has taught the powerful principles that created incredible wealth in his life and many others.

Today he serves more than 300,000 subscribers from virtually every country in the world. He's become an internationally known expert in goal achieving and hosted his own TV show, Goals 2 Go, on TSTN. His book, *13 Secrets of World Class Achievers,* is the number one goal setting book at both the Kindle store and Apple iBookstore. Another best seller, *Day by Day with James Allen,* has sold more than 75,000 copies and has been translated into Japanese, Czech, Slovak and Farsi. His three-day weekend seminar event, Claim Your Power Now, has attracted such icons as Bob Proctor, Jim Rohn, Denis Waitley and many others.

His websites include:

AsAManThinketh.net
Goals2Go.com
MyDailyInsights.com
VicJohnson.com
mp3Motivators.com
ClaimYourPowerNow.com
GettingRichWitheBooks.com
LaurenzanaPress.com

Printed in Great Britain
by Amazon

37958481R00057